Dear Parent:
Your child's love of reading starts here!

Every child learns to read in a different way and at his or her own speed.
You can help your young reader improve and become more confident
by encouraging his or her own interests and abilities. You can also guide
your child's spiritual development by reading stories with biblical values
and Bible stories, like I Can Read! books published by Zonderkidz. From
books your child reads with you to the first books he or she reads alone,
there are I Can Read! books for every stage of reading:

SHARED READING
Basic language, word repetition, and whimsical
illustrations, ideal for sharing with your emergent reader.

BEGINNING READING
Short sentences, familiar words, and simple concepts for
children eager to read on their own.

READING WITH HELP
Engaging stories, longer sentences, and language play
for developing readers.

READING ALONE
Complex plots, challenging vocabulary, and high-interest
topics for the independent reader.

ADVANCED READING
Short paragraphs, chapters, and exciting themes for the
perfect bridge to chapter books.

I Can Read! books have introduced children to the joy of reading since
1957. Featuring award-winning authors and illustrators and a fabulous
cast of beloved characters, I Can Read! books set the standard for
beginning readers.

A lifetime of discovery begins with the magical words "I Can Read!"

Visit www.icanread.com for information on enriching your child's reading experience.
Visit www.zonderkidz.com for more Zonderkidz I Can Read! titles.

I Can Read!™

BEGINNING READING 1

RUBY
Bakes a Cake

by Susan Hill
pictures by Margie Moore

A friend loves at all times.

—Proverbs 17:17

ZONDERKIDZ

Ruby Bakes a Cake

Copyright © 2004, 2010 by Susan Hill
Illustrations © 2004, 2010 by Margie Moore

Requests for information should be addressed to:

Zonderkidz, *Grand Rapids, Michigan 49530*

Library of Congress Cataloging-in-Publication Data
Long, Susan Hill
    Ruby bakes a cake / by Susan Hill ; [illustrations by Margie Moore].
       p.   cm. — (I can read book)
    Summary: Ruby Racoon asks her friends for advice on making a cake.
    ISBN 978-0-310-72022-5 (softcover)
    [1. Cake—Fiction. 2. Friendship—Fiction. 3. Raccoon—Fiction. 4. Animals—
Fiction.] I. Moore, Margie, ill. II. Title.
    PZ7.L8582Rue 2010
    [E]—dc22   2009033134

Editor: Mary Hassinger

Printed in China

10 11 12 13 14 15 /SCC/ 22 21 20 19 18 17 16 15 14 13 12 11 10 9 8 7 6 5 4 3 2 1

For Molly
—S. H.

For Jessie
—M. M.

Ruby Raccoon wanted

to bake a cake,

but she didn't know how.

"I will ask my friends

what it takes

to bake a cake," she said.

Ruby ran to the stone wall.

She saw Sam Squirrel.

"Sam, what does it take

to bake a cake?"

"Try adding nuts," said Sam.

"God bless you!" said Ruby.

"Come join me

when my cake is done!"

Ruby ran to the fence.

She saw Bunny Rabbit.

"Bunny, what does it take

to bake a cake?"

"Every cake needs carrot tops,"

said Bunny.

"God bless you!" called Ruby.

"Please come over

when my cake is done!"

Ruby ran to the brook.

She saw Dan Duck.

"Dan, what does it take

to bake a cake?"

"I have never made a cake,

but I always enjoy snails," said Dan.

"God bless you!" said Ruby.

"Please come to my house

when my cake is done!"

Ruby ran to the tree.

She saw Jenny Wren.

"Jenny, what does it take

to bake a cake?"

"Don't forget wiggly worms,"

said Jenny.

"God bless you!"

called Ruby.

"Please come over

when my cake is done!"

Ruby ran to the pond.

She saw Frankie Frog.

"Frankie, what does it take

to bake a cake?"

Flick. *Flick*. "Flies," said Frankie.

"God bless you!" said Ruby.

"Please join me

when my cake is done!"

Ruby ran home.

She put everything into a big bowl.

She mixed up the batter

and put it in a pan.

She baked it in the oven.

"This does not smell good,"

said Ruby.

Ruby's friends came to share her cake.

She took it out of the oven.

20

"This does not look good,"

said Ruby.

21

Ruby cut the cake.

The friends said a thank-you prayer.

They all began to eat.

"This does not taste good,"

said Ruby.

"No, no, Ruby,

the cake is nice and crunchy,"

said Sam.

"And the cake is good and tall,"
said Bunny.

"It has a lovely round shape,"
said Dan.

"I have never tasted
such a juicy cake,"
said Jenny.

"And what a color, Ruby!"

said Frankie.

"This is one green cake."

Ruby smiled.

"It is not a good cake," she said.

"But you are very good friends.

Thank you, God,

for friends and cake!"